W9-BIC-414

A JOLLYTOLOGIST® BOOK

TEACHERLAUGHS

A JOLLYTOLOGIST® BOOK

TeacherLaughs

Quips, Quotes, and Anecdotes about the Classroom

COMPILED BY
Allen Klein

GRAMERCY BOOKS
NEW YORK

Published by Gramercy Books, an imprint of Random House Value Publishing,
a division of Random House, Inc., New York.

Gramercy is a registered trademark and the colophon is a trademark of Random House, Inc.

Random House
New York • Toronto • London • Sydney • Auckland
www.randomhouse.com

Interior book design by Karen Ocker Design

Printed and bound in Singapore

A catalog record for this title is available from the Library of Congress.

ISBN-13: 978-0-517-22818-0
ISBN-10: 0-517-22818-1

10 9 8 7 6 5 4 3 2

CONTENTS

Acknowledgments 6
Introduction 7

Teaching Matters 11
    What I Learned in School Today 25
    Teachers Ask, Kids Answer 29
    Students Say the Silliest Things 36

Classroom Matters 43
    Preschool 49
    Kindergarten 56
    Grade School 65
    Junior High and High School 80
    College 87

Parent-Teacher Matters 99
    Show and Tell 104
    Homework 107
    Report Cards 111
    When I Went to School 113

Index 121
About the Author 128

ACKNOWLEDGMENTS

The author wishes to thank the following writers for their contribution to this book:

Joan Clayton, author of *Teacher—We Love Your Class*

Ron Dentinger, author of *Down Time*

Patricia Harrington, author of *Death Comes Too Soon*

Liz Curtis Higgs, author of *While Shepherds Washed Their Flocks*

Grace Witwer Housholder, author of *The Funny Things Kids Say* series

Steve Kissell, author of *Surviving Life with Laughter*

INTRODUCTION

I have had many great teachers in my life.

Teachers like Mr. Elson and Mr. London, at Hunter College, who helped me pursue my dream of being a stage designer. They encouraged me, guided me, and were instrumental in getting me into Yale Drama School, which led to an almost ten-year stint at CBS television designing shows for Captain Kangaroo, Merv Griffin, and Jackie Gleason.

Teachers like Stephen Levine, who helped me find my spiritual path. His discussions about loss one minute and laughing about it the next led me further down the path of investigating the connection between humor and death, and the publication of my book *The Courage to Laugh*.

There were other great teachers in my life too. I wish there were some way I could track them down and personally thank them for their wisdom, their encouragement, and their guidance. Since that is impossible, I offer this book to them, and to all teachers, as both a tribute and a "thank you" for the wonderful work they do.

ALLEN KLEIN,
SAN FRANCISCO

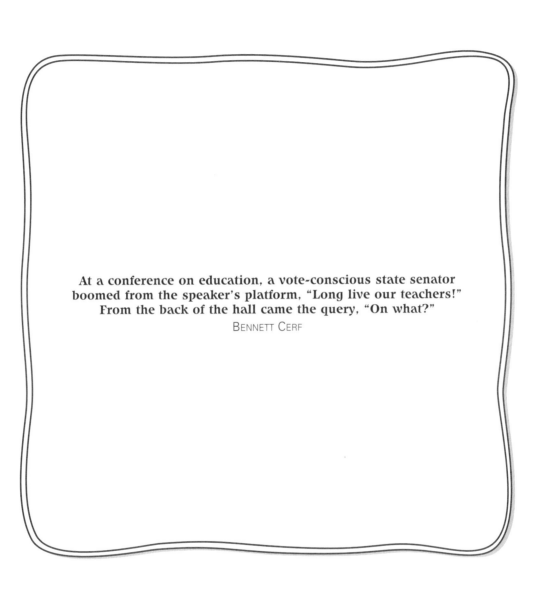

At a conference on education, a vote-conscious state senator
boomed from the speaker's platform, "Long live our teachers!"
From the back of the hall came the query, "On what?"

BENNETT CERF

WHAT I LEARNED IN SCHOOL TODAY

TEACHING

MATTERS

TEACHERS ASK, KIDS ANSWER

STUDENTS SAY THE SILLIEST THINGS

teach´er n. —the grown-up at the front of the classroom who has a collection of mugs, trophies, and plaques gathering dust in the closet at home.

RICK DETORIE

A teacher is someone who can drink three cups of coffee before eight in the morning and hold it until three in the afternoon.

ANONYMOUS

Reasons to Be a Teacher:

- You want your summers free so you can scrape together a living by driving a cab, tending bar, and selling Fuller brushes.

- You are a natural actor, unfazed by an audience that eats Fritos, applies nail polish, and creaks Double Bubble during your performance.

- You want to impress your friends—particularly those under age eleven.

- You love moron jokes.

- You have neat handwriting.

ART PETERSON

A country school board was interviewing a potential teacher.
In questioning him, one board member asked whether the
earth was round or flat. The teacher didn't bat an eye.
"I don't know how you people feel about it," he said,
"but I can teach it either way."

ANONYMOUS

A teacher is a person who
used to think he liked children.

JOEY ADAMS

I taught Sunday school for two years
and I got fired. I abused my authority. I used to
teach class like this: "Okay, if one more person talks,
everybody is going to hell." I used to keep a list up
on the board of who was going to burn.

MARGARET CHO

You Know You're A Teacher When . . .

- Your own children raise their hand in order to speak at the dinner table.

- You have programmed yourself to say sweetie or honey instead of #@?!!*@?

- You dream of decorating bulletin boards.

- You have to leave town to buy your underwear 'cause your former students are checkout clerks at your favorite stores.

- When you tell your spouse every move you make such as, "I'm going to the bathroom now and I'll be right back. Okay?"

TEACHERSZINE.COM

You know you've been teaching too long when you assign seats at dinner and ask everybody to sign their place mats in the upper right hand corner.

AN APPLE A DAY PERPETUAL CALENDAR

When I was teaching special education, it was sometimes embarrassing to run into children from my school in the supermarket or at the mall. Invariably, I would hear a boy or girl shout across the store, "Hey, look. There's the retarded teacher from my school!"

I preferred to call myself a special ed teacher. However, even that had its disadvantages. When my son David was about four, I brought him to school with me to visit the special ed classes I had been talking about. He interacted with each child at some point during the day and seemed very interested in both the activities and the children. On the ride home, I asked him if he had any questions about my class.

"Just one," he said. "Which one was Ed?"

ELAINE LUNDBERG

You Know You're a Teacher When . . .

- You believe the staff room should have a Valium salt lick.
- You want to slap the next person who says, "Must be nice to have all your holidays and summers free."
- You can tell it's a full moon without ever looking outside.
- You believe in aerial spraying of Prozac.
- You think caffeine should be available in intravenous form.

ANONYMOUS

**One teacher I know claims there are only
two reasons for being a teacher—July and August.**

ANONYMOUS

No wonder the teacher knows so much; she has the book.

EDGAR WATSON HOWE

**Lunch monitor, playground supervisor, bathroom guard:
It's a good thing I invested in four years of college!**

AN APPLE A DAY PERPETUAL CALENDAR

**A teacher's day is one-half bureaucracy, one-half crises,
one-half monotony, and one-eightieth epiphany.
Never mind the arithmetic.**

SUSAN OHANIAN

**Teachers are much more candid than they used to be. During
Open School week, I walked up to a teacher who was watching
two six-year-olds yelling and screaming and jumping up and
down on a seesaw. I said, "Aren't they something?"
She said, "Yes, I wish I had a dozen like them."
I said, "How many do you have?" She said, "Three dozen."**

ROBERT ORBEN, *2400 JOKES TO BRIGHTEN YOUR SPEECHES*

We should not permit prayer to be taken out of school;
that's the only way most of us get through.

SAM LEVENSON

In a discussion of family units, one day, the conversation turned to twins. I told the students that I had a twin brother who was also a teacher, and if they wished, I would ask him to be their teacher the following Monday. The kids were so excited! I was also really excited, but for a different reason: I don't have a twin brother! When Monday arrived, I dressed in a suit and tie, slicked back my hair with a new part on the side, and wore my old glasses. When the students first saw me, they were very shy. Some were nonbelievers; however, I quickly convinced them that I was my twin brother by calling them incorrect names and having to use nametags. When it came time to collect homework that had been assigned to them on Friday, they informed me that my "brother" had said nothing about it! When Tuesday arrived and I asked the children for their homework, they replied, "Your brother said we didn't have any homework, and we like him better!"

STEVE KISSELL

The school system has a way of turning nice, middle-class conformists into raging wackos. No one is immune. One moment you'll be routinely filling out your "Request for an Order Request Form," and the next moment you'll be trying to eat the chalk tray. So pay attention to these clues that suggest you may be losing your grip:

- You read over old administrative memos, looking for insights into the meaning of life.

- You suddenly begin to savor the coffee in the school cafeteria.

- You throw caution to the wind and request two staplers in one semester.

ART PETERSON

Is it any wonder that teaching is considered one of the most stressful professions? For example, one of my teachers was a recent college graduate. As the school year progressed, . . . she began to develop ulcers, so under her doctor's recommendation, she asked for a leave of absence. Surprisingly, she chose to visit a Latin American country, which, at the time, was going through a lot of turmoil. We didn't hear from her for two or three months, but then this letter arrived.

Dear Faculty,

   I've got good news and bad news. The bad news is that on the way to my vacation, the plane was hijacked, and it was flown to a little grass strip out in the middle of this country, and a guerrilla leader commandeered me. My life has really changed. All day long I spend my time dodging snipers taking potshots at me and driving trucks full of explosives across minefields. It's really different.

   The good news is my ulcers have cleared up!

LOU PAGE

When a teacher calls a boy by his entire name,
it means trouble.

MARK TWAIN

My students are always asking me: "How old are you?"

My standard answer is that I am older than dirt. I was born before there was electricity. Most of the time, the kids chuckle.

Last year, I was approached by an 8th grade English teacher. She wanted to know what I had been telling my students. Seems that after leaving my math class, they went to English and interrupted the discussion there by asking if the teacher knew when electricity had been invented. She said, "I'm not sure— maybe the 1880's—when Ben Franklin flew the kite . . . ." After a few more minutes of whispering with their heads together, one of the boys exclaimed, "She CAN'T be THAT old!" . . . . And they told their teacher what I had said.

She informed them that I was just fooling around with them, but they said, "NO, she was very serious."

The next day my students claimed, "You couldn't be older than electricity, 'cause then you would know Ben Franklin." I calmly replied, "Of course I knew him. Who do you think gave him the idea to fly the kite in the storm? And did I get any credit? Noooooooo... you don't see my name in the history books."

I thought for sure they would understand from my tone of voice that I was being facetious. But they returned to English and asked for permission to go to the library to check on the actual dates for the discovery of electricity.

It took a while for us to convince them that I was joking. They took it so seriously.

TEACHERS.NET/CHATBOARD

20

She used to be a schoolteacher
but she has no class now.
FRED ALLEN

I just read about a schoolteacher who got hurt.
She was grading papers on a curve.
MILTON BERLE, *MILTON BERLE'S PRIVATE JOKE FILE*

Things to Think about While Grading Papers

- Why is it that every time I count the papers in this pile, there are three more?
- I know she didn't write this, but it's too bad to be plagiarized.
- Should I write, "Why not hand in the Cliff Notes and avoid the middleman?" or would that be unprofessional?

ART PETERSON

Teacher: Someone who swore she would starve before teaching, and who has been doing both ever since.

ANONYMOUS

There was a nice boy with a very low I.Q. into whose head the teachers had been trying for many years to stuff some education, but without success. Finally, the boy left school and in a short time word came back that he had turned out to be a success on Broadway as a professional dancer. His former Principal, reporting it to the faculty, declared, "That boy didn't fail. We failed. We were trying to educate the wrong end!"

HYMAN ALPERN, *TEACHERS ARE FUNNY*

A mother was having difficulty persuading her son to go to school one morning.

"Nobody at school likes me," he cried. "The teachers don't like me. The kids pick on me all the time. I'm not going to school today!"

"You have to go to school, son," insisted his mother. "Besides, you are 40 years old. You're the principal. You have to go to school!"

ANONYMOUS

Principal to visitor: "Don't get upset if you hear the girls discussing the pill. They're talking about me."

HERB TRUE

 Old principals never die;
they just lose their faculties.

HARRY ALLEN

Some kids want to know why the teachers get paid
when it's the kids who have to do all the work!

MILTON BERLE, *MILTON BERLE'S PRIVATE JOKE FILE*

Do you know the difference between education and experience?
Education is what you get when you read the fine print.
Experience is what you get when you don't.

PETE SEEGER

Education can get you the only thing that really matters
in today's world—an assigned parking space.

GENE PERRET

How is it that little children are so intelligent and men
so stupid? It must be education that does it.

ALEXANDER DUMAS

If you think education is expensive—try ignorance.

DEREK BOK

As a teacher, I tried to make my lesson plans relate to real life. It's
important for kids to see connections. "Johnny, you got a sixty-five
on this test. That's a D, and it's also the speed limit on the
freeway! Uh oh, Suzie got the speed limit in a residential area."

LESLEY WAKE

Visitor: You must have an unusually bright class. Whenever you asked a question—no matter how difficult—every student raised his hand.

Teacher: No, they are just average students. Confidentially, the explanation for their hand-raising is that whenever we have a visitor, all students raise their hands. Those who know the answer raise the right hand; those who don't know the answer raise the left hand.

HYMAN ALPERN, *TEACHERS ARE FUNNY*

Lesson plans: Formal outlines written two weeks after the lesson has been taught.

Staff meetings: The time you're allotted to do your lesson plans.

DIANE LOOMANS AND KAREN KOLBERG

The secret of teaching is to appear to have known all your life what you learned this afternoon.

ANONYMOUS

If Columbus had an advisory committee, he would probably still be at the dock.

ARTHUR GOLDBERG

In the first place, God made idiots. That was for practice.
Then he made school boards.

MARK TWAIN

If a doctor, lawyer, or dentist had forty people in his office at one time, all of whom had different needs, and some of whom didn't want to be there and were causing trouble, and the doctor, lawyer, or dentist, without assistance, had to treat them all with professional excellence for nine months, then he might have some conception of the classroom teacher's job.

DONALD D. QUINN

WHAT I LEARNED IN SCHOOL TODAY

A child comes home from his first day at school.
His mother asks, "What did you learn today?"
The child replies, "Not enough. I have to go back tomorrow."

ANONYMOUS

When a kindergarten student was asked what she
had learned the first day in school, she said: "First of all,
I learned that my name isn't 'Pumpkin'—it's 'Karla.'"

ANONYMOUS

A seven-year-old was giving his younger
brother advice on starting school. "Whatever you do,
don't learn to spell 'cat'—because if you do, after
that the words just get harder and harder."

ANONYMOUS

Elroy came home from his first day at school.
"Nothing much happened," he told his mother. "Some lady
didn't know how to spell 'cat.' I told her."

JOSEPH ROSENBLOOM, *696 SILLY SCHOOL JOKES & RIDDLES*

A little girl had just finished her first week of school.
"I'm wasting my time," she said to her mother. "I can't read,
I can't write—and they won't let me talk!"

BECQUET.COM

"Well," said Mrs. Jones to her young daughter, "and what did you learn in Sunday school today?"

"We learned," said little Nancy, "about Moses."

"Ah," said her mother, "and what did you learn about Moses?"

Nancy said, "Well, he was a general leading an army on a retreat from Egypt. The Egyptians, in hot pursuit, had the weight of tanks on their side, and Moses, taking casualties, was forced back upon the Red Sea, where he faced annihilation. Calling for air cover, however, he proceeded to throw a pontoon bridge hastily across—"

By this time, Mrs. Jones had finally managed to catch her breath and said, "Nancy! Surely that is not what they taught you about Moses."

27

"Well, not exactly," said Nancy, "but if I told it to you the way the teacher told it to me, you'd never believe it."

ISAAC ASIMOV, *ASIMOV LAUGHS AGAIN*

"I won a prize in kindergarten today," a boy boasted to his mother. "Teacher asked me how many legs a hippopotamus has, and I said 'three.'"

"Three?" said his mother. "How on earth could you have won the prize?"

"I came the closest," the boy said.

ART LINKLETTER

A Sunday school teacher was discussing the Ten Commandments with her five and six year olds. After explaining the commandment to "honor" thy Father and thy Mother, she asked, "Is there a commandment that teaches us how to treat our brothers and sisters?" Without missing a beat one little boy answered, "Thou shall not kill."

ANONYMOUS

"How did school go today?" a mother inquired of her son.

"Fine," the little fellow replied. "We had a new teacher. She wanted to know if I had any sisters or brothers and I told her I was an only child."

"What did she say?" his mother asked.

"She said, 'Thank goodness.'"

ANONYMOUS

28

Yesterday, our 10-year-old got home from school and we were talking about what he had done during the day. He told us that Tuesday is art class day for his class and that they talked about a famous painter, but he could not remember the artist's name. My wife asked if the artist was Grandma Moses.

Our son replied in a huff: "No, Mom, it wasn't one of your relatives."

WARNING! CUTE KID STORIES AHEAD!

A mother was putting away dishes in the kitchen when she heard her son call from the den, "Mom, come quickly. I learned how to make babies in school today."

She almost dropped the dishes and had just composed herself when he again called, "Mom, come and see what I learned about making babies."

When she finally arrived, her son beamed enthusiastically and said, "See, Mom, you can change the *y* to *i* and add *es* to make *babies*."

RICHARD LEDERER

TEACHERS ASK, KIDS ANSWER

When the arithmetic teacher asked, "If you reached in one pocket and pulled out 20 cents and you reached in another pocket and pulled out 80 cents—what would you have?" The student answered, "Somebody else's pants."

PHYLLIS DILLER

Teacher:	That's quite a cough you have there. What are you taking for it?
Pupil:	I don't know, teacher. What will you give me?

Teacher:	Class, someone has stolen my purse out of my desk. It had $100 in it. I know you're all basically good kids, so I'm willing to offer a reward of $10 to whoever returns it.
Voice at the back of the room:	I'm offering $20!

ILANA WEITZMAN, EVA BLANK, AND ROSEANNE GREEN, *JOKELOPEDIA*

I hated math. Math teachers would ask me the question, "Mr. Kinney, can you tell us the common denominator here?"
  Yeah, we all think this sucks.

DAVID KINNEY

Teacher:	If you add 43,584 + 22,979, divide the answer by 5, and multiply by 3, what do you get?
Student:	The wrong answer!

ANONYMOUS

30

Teacher: If $1+1=2$ and $2+2=4$, what is $4+4$?

Student: That's not fair! You answer all the easy ones and give us the hard one.

ANONYMOUS

The boy's impatient math teacher snarled, "And just how far are you from the correct answer?" To which the boy replied, "Three seats."

JEFF ROVIN

Teacher: Can you count to 10?

Suzanne: Yes, teacher. (counting on her fingers at waist level) One, two, three, four, five, six, seven, eight, nine, ten.

Teacher: Good. Now can you count higher?

Suzanne: Yes, teacher. (She puts her hands over her head and counts on her fingers.) One, two, three, four, five, six, seven, eight, nine, ten.

JOSEPH ROSENBLOOM, *696 SILLY SCHOOL JOKES & RIDDLES*

The teacher asked, "Tell me, Johnny, if I had nine apples and there were twelve children, how would I divide them equally?"

Johnny thought for a moment, then replied happily, "Make applesauce!"

HELEN RUDIN

The math teacher saw that little Johnny wasn't paying attention in class. She called on him and said, "Johnny! What are 2 and 4 and 28 and 44?"

Little Johnny quickly replied, "NBC, CBS, HBO, and the Cartoon network!"

ANONYMOUS

The teacher told my kid, "An apple a day keeps the doctor away." He said, "What do you got for cops?"

RODNEY DANGERFIELD

Student: My science teacher says I should be an oceanographer.

Dad: Really, why?

Student: Because all my grades are below C level.

ANONYMOUS

Teacher: Joseph, give me the formula for water.

Joseph: I, J, K L, M, N, O.

Teacher: That is not correct.

Joseph: I thought that was right. After all, you said the formula was H to O.

ANONYMOUS

Question: Who was Magellan?

Answer: The man who circumsized [sic] the world.

• • •

Question: Describe "The Last Supper."

Answer: It is Jesus and the twelve apostrophes having their last meal together.

• • •

Question: Give the days of the week in French.

Answer: Lundi, Mardi, Mecredi, Vasectomy

BREEDING AS A SPORT: 101 STUDENT HOWLERS

33

Teacher: Tell me a sentence with a direct object.
Student: Teacher, you're beautiful.
Teacher: What's the object?
Student: An "A."

ANONYMOUS

Answer briefly: Why do we study *The Myths* and *The Odyssey?*

• Because we want to talk like cultured people. At a party how would you like it if someone mentioned a Greek god and you didn't know him. You would be embarrassed.

• If it wasn't for Myths where would Shakesper [sic] be today?

• We read it because it's a classicle.

BEL KAUFMAN

The suffix "-ous" means "full of." For example, "joyous" means "full of joy," "pompous" means "full of pomp," and many other similar words. Now, can you give me another example?

"Pious."

HYMAN ALPERN, *TEACHERS ARE FUNNY*

A specialist came to the classroom to conduct academic evaluations. Nathan was the first one in line.

"When is your birthday?" the specialist asked.

"October 16," he answered.

"What year?"

He sighed, then replied, "Every year."

JUDY MOON DENSON AND BEVERLY SMALLWOOD, *KIDSPIRATION*

Having been a competitive gymnast, I'm a stickler on form. Some time ago I was teaching a class of three and four year olds. I demonstrated a forward roll, explaining every move until the roll was fully executed. "Now," I said, "I want you to do exactly what I just did. Do you have any questions?"

A wide-eyed youngster timidly raised her hand. "Miss Michele," she asked, "how do we make our knees crack?"

| Teacher: | Johnny, please spell the word "Mississippi." |
| Johnny: | The river or the state? |

• • •

| Teacher: | I told you to stand at the end of the line! |
| Pupil: | I tried, but there was someone already there! |

• • •

| Teacher: | Do you know Lincoln's Gettysburg address? |
| Pupil: | No, I believe he moved. |

ANONYMOUS

The teacher was trying to impress upon her pupils the importance of doing right at all times, and to bring out the answer "bad habits." She inquired: "What is it that we find so easy to get into and so hard to get out of?"

There was silence for a moment and then one little fellow answered "Bed."

LEWIS AND FAYE COPELAND, *10,000 JOKES, TOASTS & STORIES*

STUDENTS SAY THE SILLIEST THINGS

Teachers not only perform vitally important functions in our society; they are also great straight men.

"Are your mother and father in?" asked one instructor when a small boy opened the door.

"Well," said the boy, "They was in but they is out now."

"They was in? they is out?" said the shocked teacher. "Where is your grammar?"

"Oh," said the boy, "She's upstairs takin' a bath."

STEVE ALLEN, *STEVE ALLEN'S PRIVATE JOKE FILE*

"Do you know what happened in 1492?" I asked a boy of nine.

"Oh, *somethin'* happened," he brightly said.

"Yes, it was that kind of year: Things were happening every day. But I'm thinking of something *special* that happened in 1492 that didn't happen in 1926."

"Fourteen ninety-two... fourteen ninety-two . . . "

He was saying it as if expecting a snap from center.

"I'll give you a hint: It was a famous year in American history," I said, now so confused by the kids that I'd forgotten there *was* no American history in 1492.

"The Declaration of Independence was signed?"

"No, they were still working on it, but something special *was* discovered that year."

I expected him to say "penicillin."

"Yeah!" he cried. "Frozen yogurt!"

BILL COSBY

"All right, everybody on their backs with their feet up in the air!" the gym teacher shouted to his third-grade class. "I want you to pretend you're riding a bicycle."

Dropping to the floor, the students began rapidly kicking their legs in the sky—all except for one boy who slowly moved one foot in the air while the other leg lay limp on the floor.

"What's wrong with you?" asked the gym teacher.

"Isn't it obvious?" said the boy. "I've got a flat."

MATT RISSINGER AND PHILIP YATES, *BIGGEST JOKE BOOK IN THE WORLD*

I offer my favorite student howlers, each a certifiably pure and priceless gem of fractured English worthy of a Pullet Surprise:

- A virgin forest is a place where the hand of man had never set foot.
- Running is a unique experience, and I thank God for exposing me to the track team.
- When you breathe, you inspire. When you do not breathe, you expire.

RICHARD LEDERER

- The part I enjoyed most at sports days was the tug of whore.
- It was Nathan Haley who said: "I only regret that I have but one life to lose for my country." This has come to be known as the famous Haley's comment.

BREEDING AS A SPORT: 101 STUDENT HOWLERS

- An appendix is something found in the back of a book. Sometimes they get in people and have to be taken out.
- There are some things about electricity we still are not sure of. These things are called whats.
- To protect the North American Indians, the government put them in reservoirs.

THE WORLD ACCORDING TO KIDS

I am sitting at my desk taking roll and collecting the usual morning notes. One of my students walks over to give me a note from his mother and tells me she is a hairdresser. I reply, "That's nice." Then he asks me if my hair is really red. I ask him why he is asking.

Very politely he tells me, "My Mom can fix those roots for you at a very good price."

TEACHERSZINE.COM

My neighbor, a primary-school teacher,
asked one of her pupils, an adopted child, how
he felt about his mother's pregnancy. "Wonderful," the
student replied. "And this is her first baby from scratch!"

BECQUET.COM

We had a teacher in school who hated kids—he caught me reading a comic book in class and snatched it away from me. "You'll get this back at the end of the semester."

"Why, is it gonna take you that long to read it?"

BILL COSBY

The new Vice Principal made an announcement over the school intercom: "The staff and students would like to congratulate Mr. Green on his forthcoming marriage."

Later, when she saw him he thanked her for the special attention. He added, that perhaps, for junior high school, she should use smaller words. It seems two or three students had asked him about his three earlier marriages.

ANONYMOUS

40

A teacher asked her class, "In ancient times some people believed that a certain heroic figure supported the earth on his shoulders. What was the name of this personage?"

"Atlas," said a little girl.

"That is correct," said the teacher, "but if Atlas carried the earth on his shoulders, how was Atlas supported?"

"Maybe," the little girl said, "his old lady took in washing."

The same history teacher asked, "Where was the Declaration of Independence signed?"

A bright youngster replied, "At the bottom."

STEVE ALLEN, *STEVE ALLEN'S PRIVATE JOKE FILE*

I was called into a meeting with my team of teachers to talk with Jimmy about his language and yelling in the class. Jimmy was complaining to us, "That girl wouldn't stop mess'n with me. She keeps on looking at me and I don't like it." The thought that she might like him never came into his mind. He yelled out across the room to the girl, "If you don't quit I'm gonna hit you with my FEE-SEES." We weren't really sure Jimmy knew what he said, so we played it cool and asked Jimmy to slowly explain what he meant and was it a real threat.

Jimmy, very upset that we are not dealing with her and assuming we are so dumb because we don't know what FEE-SEES is. He slowly acts out what he wanted to do. He grabs his leg, holds up his foot and then while waving his foot says, "I'm gonna hit you with my TWO FEE-SEES (FEETS)." We promptly held back the laughter and then assigned him extra language arts homework on irregular plural nouns.

41

"If you were president, what would you do?"

"I'd change the law so there was only school from nine to ten in the morning," she replied.

"That long, eh?"

"That's enough school."

"What about recess? That used to be my favorite subject."

"Well, you wouldn't go *all* the way from nine to ten. You'd have to have recess too."

"And lunch?"

"Oh, sure, lunch."

"So you'd really be going for about twenty minutes."

"That's fine with *me*."

BILL COSBY

One day the teacher gave a true-false test. One student reached into his pocket, dug out a coin, and flipped it for each answer. Heads for true and tails for false.

After the test, when the rest of the class had left the room, the student was still flipping the coins.

"What's taking you so long to finish the test?" the teacher asked.

"Oh, I finished a while ago," the student said. "Now I'm just checking my answers."

ANONYMOUS

PRESCHOOL

KINDERGARTEN

GRADE SCHOOL

CLASSROOM MATTERS

JUNIOR HIGH AND HIGH SCHOOL

COLLEGE

[School is] a kind of state-supported baby-sitting service.

GERALD KENNEDY

How do you explain "counterclockwise" to a child with a digital watch?

ANONYMOUS

How do you write zero in Roman numerals?

GEORGE CARLIN

She doesn't understand the concept of Roman numerals. She thought we just fought World War Eleven.

JOAN RIVERS

Bad Spellers of the world UNTIE!

BUMPER STICKER

The teacher was annoyed with her students, who kept checking the clock on the wall. She covered it with a sign that read, "Time will pass. Will you?"

JOSEPH ROSENBLOOM, *696 SILLY SCHOOL JOKES & RIDDLES*

Some students drink at the fountain of knowledge.
Others just gargle.

E. C. McKenzie, *14,000 Quips and Quotes for Writers and Speakers*

Where do students sit when they are learning math?
At multiplication tables.

• • •

What kind of school would you find on top of a mountain?
A high school.

• • •

How did the teacher unlock the door to the music room?
With a piano key.

Marilyn Helmer and Jane Kurisu, *Recess Riddles*

"And how many hours a day did you do lessons?" asked Alice, in
a hurry to change the subject.

"Ten hours the first day," said the Mock Turtle: "nine the next,
and so on."

"What a curious plan!" exclaimed Alice.

"That's the reason they're called lesson," the Gryphon remarked:
"because they lessen from day to day."

Lewis Carroll

Teacher: "Can" is whether you're capable of doing something. "May" is asking for permission.

(Responding to a student's raised hand) Yes, Michael.

Michael: Can I go to the bathroom?

Teacher: Michael, do you want to repeat the question?

Michael: (To himself) Oh, no. I'm going to be made an example of.

Teacher: Michael!

Michael: I said, "Can I go to the bathroom?"

Teacher: You can, but you *may* not.

Michael: Well, can I or can't I?

Teacher: I don't think you've been paying attention. Have you, Michael Kaye?

Michael: Yes, I have.

Teacher: So, how would you rephrase the question?

Michael: Can I *please* go to the bathroom? (class laughs)

Teacher: Children! . . . Michael Kaye, why don't you just spend some time in the hallway until you've learned the difference between "can" and "may."
(To Michael leaving the room) When you've learned the difference, then you *may* come back in.

Another
student: (Whispering to a fellow student) I have to go to the bathroom but I'm afraid to ask.

BARRY LEVINSON, *AVALON*

My teacher has a reading problem.
He can't read my writing.
LEOPOLD FECHTNER

```
 O | X
---------
 X | O
---------
   | X
```

I'm thirty years old but I read at the thirty-four-year level.
DANA CARVEY

Sex education may be a good idea in the schools
but I don't believe the kids should be given homework.
BILL COSBY

They say teaching sex education in the public schools
will promote promiscuity. With our educational system?
If we promote promiscuity the same way we promote math
or science, they've got nothing to worry about.
BEVERLY MICKINS

One student asked her friend, "Have you read any mysteries lately?"
"Yes." her friend said, "I'm reading one now."
"What's the title?"
"Advanced Algebra."
WINSTON K. PENDLETON, *COMPLETE SPEAKER'S GALAXY OF*
FUNNY STORIES, JOKES AND ANECDOTES

My daughter is taking an advanced English class.
She's reading a book that wasn't even written yet.

DAVE COOPERBERG

Don't let your child stay home every time
he complains he is sick. Why do you think they have
ambulances? To take a kid to school, regardless.

PHYLLIS DILLER

Any student will tell you that the longest five minutes in the
world are the last five minutes of a lecture, while the shortest
five minutes are the last five minutes of an exam.

KARL NEWELL

The schoolmaster stood with his back to the fireplace on a winter
morning, and addressed good advice to the pupils before starting
the day's lessons.

"Before you speak, think. Count fifty before you say anything
important—a hundred, if it is very important."

The lips of his pupils were moving in unison, and suddenly
they burst out in chorus.

"Ninety-nine, one hundred! Your coattails are on fire, sir!"

ANONYMOUS

Take it from a kid, when you drive past a school playground and see a bunch of kids laughing and giggling and swinging from the jungle gym—jumping around, playing games, blowing bubble gum, telling jokes—don't think this is what we are really like.

This is just recess.

JANE WAGNER

PRESCHOOL

Are You A True Preschool Teacher?

- Do you ask guests if they have remembered their scarves and mittens as they leave your home?

- Do you move your dinner partner's glass away from the edge of the table?

- Do you ask if anyone needs to go to the bathroom as you enter a theater with a group of friends?

- Do you hand a tissue to anyone who sneezes?

- Do you say everything twice? I mean, do you repeat everything?

ANONYMOUS

The preschool teacher said, "—And that's why we all love America. Everyone in our country is free."

"Not me," said one child. "I'm four!"

LEO ROSTEN, *LEO ROSTEN'S GIANT BOOK OF LAUGHTER*

My daughter-in-law picked up her four-year-old Jamie and his little sister Suzie from daycare. Jamie was fuming. His teacher had asked what day it was. He confidently raised his hand and answered "Wednesday," only to be told it was Tuesday. He said, "Mom, you put the wrong day-of-the-week socks on Suzie and made me mess up."

BETTY BEAMGUARD

50

ODE TO CHILD CARE

Little children come to me for hugs and books and such,
I care for all their simple needs and I also fix them lunch,
I pick up toys, mop up spills and often dry their tears,
I change their diapers, settle fights, and kiss away their fears.
I tie their shoes, button coats and push them on the swing,
I really love these kids, you see, but there is just one thing,
Call me Mom, or Aunt or Donna; those names might fit,
But please don't call me "sitter," because I never get to sit.

ANONYMOUS

Preschool teacher Mrs. Kelley instructs her children to sit like pretzels with their legs crossed during story time. That way everyone is seated on the floor and everyone can see.

Grant, 5, was sitting with his legs straight out in front of him.

"Don't you know what a pretzel looks like?" Mrs. Kelley asked Grant.

"But Mrs. Kelley," he said. "I like straight pretzels!"

GRACE WITWER HOUSHOLDER

During an Open House at our school, I heard one mother, trying to get her four-year-old to eat her meal, say, "Susie, your peas are saying, 'Eat me! Eat Me!'" The tiny girl stared at the peas and slowly picked up her fork. As she methodically began mashing each one, she muttered, "Shut up, peas!"

THE WORLD ACCORDING TO KIDS

Reasons to Become a Preschool Teacher:

- Cute little children . . . Cute little paycheck.
- Confidence that you will never, ever forget to count to 10.
- Shoes that untie themselves.
- Get to sing your favorite songs over and over and over.
- Small hands . . . LARGE crayons.

ANONYMOUS

I took my preschool class and some of their siblings out to the Kelowna Airport to greet the Queen. The parent-helpers and I had to supervise close to fifty excited children. They had all brought lunches, books, and toys to keep themselves occupied during the two-hour wait. It was difficult to stay together in such a vast crowd, and one five-year-old became quite concerned when he couldn't find his older brother. I told him that his brother was perfectly safe with one of the helpers, so he didn't have to worry about him. "Yes, I do!" the child exclaimed indignantly. "He's got our lunch!"

One day, after a group discussion about family celebrations, one little boy in my preschool class raised his hand. He said, "My family celebrates Lent."

A girl sitting next to him said, "What's that?"

He very seriously replied, "You know, that fuzzy stuff in your dryer."

VALEKA PETERSON

While a preschool teacher was taking a station wagon full of kids home one day, a fire truck drove past. In the front was a pair of Dalmatian dogs. This brought up a discussion of why the firemen have dogs.

"They use them to keep crowds back," one youngster said.

"No," said another, "they are just for good luck."

A third child's response brought the argument to a close. "They use the dogs," she said, "to find the fire hydrant."

ANONYMOUS

One daycare school administrator wanted to know more about his students' hobbies. So he asked a group of them what they do after school.

One of the youngsters replied, "I go home."

ANONYMOUS

In case I'm ever asked to give a commencement address for a preschool graduation, I've created a list of all the important rules every five-year-old should know: (excerpted)

Don't be afraid to ask where the restroom is.

Flush.

Wear your jacket outside on a cold day, even if it covers up your Batman cape.

Don't bother mixing purple and orange paint.

Don't lick your glue stick.

DEBBIE FARMER

Jasmine, 4, was very excited about attending preschool. One day when her mother asked the usual, "How was school today?" she sadly replied that it was not a good day. "Why?" her mother asked.

"My teacher said I have TWO moms," Jasmine said.

"What?!" her mother said.

"I drew a picture for you," Jasmine explained, "and she said to write 'TWO MOM' on it." Then Jasmine handed her mother the picture which had the words 'WON MOM' (one mom) written across it.

"Oh, I see," her mother said. "Your teacher wanted you to write 'To: Mom.' That means 'for mom.'"

Jasmine replied in utter confusion, "You mean I have FOUR MOMS?"

GRACE STOKES

At the end of the school year, an evaluation was done to decide whether Tristan would continue in a learning disabled class or could be mainstreamed into a normal kindergarten.

One test was a series of questions to determine his social skills. The tester asked, "What do you say to people when you are in their home and you accidentally break something that belongs to them?"

Tristan looked at his mother, Monical and his older brother, Austin. Then he turned to his teacher and, in his clearest voice, said. "I say 'Austin did it!'"

MARGARET G. BIGGER, *MOTHERHOOT*

Steven's preschool class went on a field trip to the fire station. The firefighter giving the presentation held up a smoke detector and asked the class: "Does anyone know what this is?" Steven's hand shot up and the firefighter called on him. Steven replied: "That's how Mommy knows supper is ready!"

MARTHA MILES

KINDERGARTEN

**A kindergarten teacher has to know how
to make the little things count.**

HENNY YOUNGMAN

Thirty minutes after the opening bell of the first day of kindergarten, Charles's teacher noticed that he was packing up all of his things and putting them back into his school bag.

"Charles, what are you doing?" she asked.

"I'm going home," he replied.

"You can't go home now! We're going to be here until 2:30 this afternoon."

He looked the teacher squarely in the eye and asked, *"Who signed me up for this?"*

JUDY MOON DENSON AND BEVERLY SMALLWOOD, *KIDSPIRATION*

When Darrell was in kindergarten, he said me instead of I. After class one day, he said to his teacher, "Mrs. Frank, me can't put my coat on."

Mrs. Frank replied, "No, Darrell, I can't put my coat on, I can't put my coat on, I can't put my coat on."

Darrell shrugged. "That's okay, Mrs. Frank, me can't do it neither. Me go get Donna to do it for me."

LIZ CURTIS HIGGS

It was little Jeannine's first day at school. The teacher was busy getting acquainted with her new students and arranging for seating them properly. "Here," she said to Jeannine, "You may sit in this front row seat for the present."

When little Jeannine was telling her mother about it that evening, she said, "And I sat there all day and the teacher never did give me the present."

WINSTON K. PENDLETON, COMPLETE SPEAKER'S GALAXY
OF FUNNY STORIES, JOKES AND ANECDOTES

About 18 years ago, when our daughter and I went to her one-on-one kindergarten orientation, . . . her teacher was telling us all about how her half-day would be spent and discussing curriculum with me.

The kindergarten room had its own little lavatory, and near the end of the interview, the teacher, trying to familiarize our daughter with the new facilities, said to Jennifer: "Jennifer, can you show your mommy how you flush the toilet and wash your hands?"

To which my daughter politely but tentatively responded: "But . . . my mommy already knows how to do that."

WARNING! CUTE KID STORIES AHEAD!

A little boy worrying through his very first day at school raised his hand for permission to go to the washroom, then returned to the class a few moments later to report that he couldn't find it. Dispatched a second time with explicit directions, he still couldn't find it. So this time the teacher asked a slightly older boy to act as a guide. Success crowned his efforts. "We finally found it," the older boy told the teacher. "He had his pants on backward."

BENNETT CERF

On the last day of kindergarten, all the children brought presents for their teacher. The florist's son handed the teacher a gift. She shook it, held it up and said, "I bet I know what it is—it's some flowers!"

"That's right!" shouted the little boy.

Then the candy store owner's daughter handed the teacher a gift. She held it up, shook it and said, "I bet I know what it is—it's a box of candy!"

"That's right!" shouted the little girl.

The next gift was from the liquor store owner's son. The teacher held it up and saw that it was leaking. She touched a drop with her finger and tasted it. "Is it wine?" she asked.

"No," the boy answered.

The teacher touched another drop to her tongue. "Is it champagne?" she asked.

"No," the boy answered.

Finally, the teacher said, "I give up. What is it?"

The boy replied, "A puppy!"

ANONYMOUS

58

One day I introduced the new word "bow-wow" before the reading lesson. When my student came to this word on that page he was reading out loud, he stopped, scratched his head and tried so hard to remember the new word. He didn't want me to tell him the new word. He finally started over at the beginning of the page and when he came to "bow-wow," he smiled broadly, being so proud that he knew this new word and loudly said, "Woof-Woof!"

JOAN CLAYTON

A kindergarten teacher had a pupil tell her he had found a frog. She inquired as to whether it was alive or dead. "Dead," she was informed.

"How do you know?" she asked.

"Because I pissed in his ear," said the child innocently.

"You did WHAT?" squealed the teacher in surprise.

"You know," explained the boy, "I leaned over and went 'Pssst'. And he didn't move."

BECQUET.COM

Letter to a parent volunteer who had done math flash cards with a class:

Dear Nora,

Thank you very much for flashing us, we sure enjoied [sic] it.

Your friend,

Jamie

BREEDING AS A SPORT: 101 STUDENT HOWLERS

When Nicholas was attending kindergarten, Jayme, 2, was anxious to repeat anything he came home with. So it was no surprise when Nicholas was learning "The Pledge of Allegiance," Jayme was determined to learn it also. One day she got to the end and with a very bold voice, and her hand on her heart, she stated, "with liberty and breakfast for all!"

LISA DELVECCHIO

Lynne from Pennsylvania had a quiet little kindergartner. Her daughter's teacher insisted the shy student would raise her hand in class "when she's good and ready."

One day, she was ready.

Officer Friendly came to the class to teach the children about saying no to drugs and alcohol. As the teacher explained after school, the young girl had finally raised her hand to tell Officer Friendly, "My mom drinks and drives."

Lynne gasped, "She did what? I don't drink and drive."

Her daughter insisted, "Yes, you do, Mom. Every day you drink your coffee when you drive me to school."

LIZ CURTIS HIGGS

"Teacher, teacher, last night my mom's waterline broke and this morning she was having contraptions!"

KINDERGARTEN STUDENT

Mrs. Hilton, the kindergarten teacher, was suddenly taken ill and a replacement was hastily found. The substitute teacher had a degree in computer science and was at a loss as to what to do with the children. She decided to tell them stories. And always, at the end of each story, she would say, "And the moral of that story is . . . ." Hearing dozens of stories, the children had sat through dozens of morals.

In a few days, Mrs. Hilton recovered from her illness and returned to her class. One of her students greeted her with a smile and said, "Teacher, I'm glad you're back. I like you better than that other teacher."

Mrs. Hilton was flattered by the child, but was curious. "Why do you like me better than the other teacher?"

The child looked into the teacher's eyes and said, "Because you don't have any morals."

LOWELL D. STREIKER, *NELSON'S BIG BOOK OF LAUGHTER*

Kindergarten Instructor: What do zebras have that no other animals have?

Tiny Tim: Little zebras.

POWERS MOULTON, *2500 JOKES FOR ALL OCCASIONS*

At the elementary school in St. Bruno, Quebec, where I work, one day, early in the year, I was assigned to substitute for the regular kindergarten teacher. I met her five-year-old pupils at the bus in front of the school, and thinking to reassure them that nothing was wrong, I said, "Children, I am Miss Epps today." Everything seemed to be fine. Before the end of the morning, however, I heard one little girl say to another sitting next to her, "She's not Miss Epps!"

"I know," the other one replied, "but she wants to be Miss Epps. Let's just pretend, shall we?"

BECQUET.COM

62

The kindergarten teacher was showing her class a page from a book which had several national flags on it. She pointed to the American flag and asked, "What flag is this?"

A little girl replied, "That's our country's flag."

"Very good," the teacher said. "And what is the name of our country?"

"'Tis of thee," the little girl said.

ANONYMOUS

When one child in kindergarten broke out with chicken pox, the teacher asked each child, "Have you ever had chicken pox?"

One boy said, "No, ma'am. But I've had goose bumps!"

LIZ CURTIS HIGGS

My son's junior kindergarten class had a class trip to go maple sugaring at a nearby park. The kids and parents all filed into a shack and took their seats among posters of maple trees and bottles of maple syrup. The park's instructor introduced herself and said, "Now boys and girls, we're going to learn about something I really love to do. What do you think that something is?"

A little girl replied, "Shopping!"

JEN SINGER

A young boy ran up to his teacher with tears in his eyes. The teacher asked, "What's wrong, dear?"

The boy said, "I just found out I'll be in school until I'm eighteen."

The teacher said, "That's not a problem. I have to stay here until I'm sixty-five."

MILTON BERLE, *MILTON BERLE'S PRIVATE JOKE FILE*

With tears in his eyes, the little boy told his kindergarten teacher that only one pair of boots was left in the classroom and they weren't his.

The teacher searched and searched, but she couldn't find any other boots. "Are you sure these boots aren't yours?" she asked.

"I'm sure," the little boy sobbed. "Mine had snow on them."

JOSEPH ROSENBLOOM, *696 SILLY SCHOOL JOKES & RIDDLES*

At Sunday School they were teaching how God created everything, including human beings. Little Johnny, a child in the kindergarten class, seemed especially intent when they told him how Eve was created out of one of Adam's ribs.

Later in the week his mother noticed him lying down as though he were ill, and said, "Johnny, what is the matter?"

Little Johnny responded, "I have a pain in my side. I think I'm going to have a wife."

A kindergarten teacher was observing her classroom of children while they were drawing. She would occasionally walk around to see each child's work. As she got to one little girl who was working diligently, she asked what the drawing was. The girl replied, "I'm drawing God."

The teacher paused and said, "But no one knows what God looks like."

Without missing a beat or looking up from her drawing, the girl replied, "They will in a minute."

Grade School

A teacher, asked why she preferred working in an elementary school, explained, "Well, I love children of all ages, but at the grade school I'm always sure of finding a parking space."

CAPPER'S WEEKLY

My students looked beautiful for "Picture Day." The little girls with their curls and fluffy dresses and the little boys with their "spike" haircuts and little bow ties were "picture perfect." As we were lining up to go to the gym for the pictures, the principal's voice suddenly came on the intercom. He told us the photographer had made a mistake in booking and would not be at our school until next week. One of my little second grade precocious girls exclaimed, "Oh no! We took a bath for nothing."

JOAN CLAYTON

Every day during summer school the children tried a different kind of meat and their teacher asked them to identify it. On a particular day deer meat was served. No one could guess what it was. Finally the teacher told her class, "O.K., I'll give you a hint. It's what your mother sometimes calls your father."

Gerald jumped up from his seat and shouted, "Don't eat it . . . don't eat it! It's jackass."

LARRY WILDE, LARRY WILDE'S LIBRARY OF LAUGHTER

In elementary school, in case of fire you have to line
up quietly in a single-file line from smallest to tallest.
What is the logic? Do tall people burn slower?

WARREN HUTCHERSON

The teacher in one of our local grade schools was showing a
facsimile of the Declaration of Independence to her pupils. It
passed from desk to desk, and finally to Luigi, a first-generation
American. The boy studied the document reverently. Then, before
passing it on, he gravely added his own signature.

KATHERINE T. FLOYD IN *KID STUFF*

The children were lined up in the cafeteria of a Catholic elementary
school for lunch. At the head of the table was a large pile of
apples. The nun made a note, and posted on the apple tray "Take
only ONE. God is watching." Moving further along the lunch line,
at the other end of the table was a large pile of chocolate chip
cookies. A child had written a note, "Take all you want. God is
watching the apples."

ANONYMOUS

Elementary school students in Berkeley [CA] are receiving class
credit for lunch. You know parents will walk around going, "My
Timmy is an exceptional child. Only eight, but he's eating at
ninth-grade level."

JAY LENO

**Students at a Chicago grade school christened
their drinking fountain "Old Faceful."**

JAMES E. MYERS

I don't know how this came up in my math class, but . . . something about driving prompted me to tell my students that my 16-year-old daughter had just gotten her permit during the summer. Only instead of saying "permit," I said "PERIOD."

My eighth graders just stared at me as I realized that what I had just said hadn't sounded exactly right. But I didn't realize what I had said. I asked, 'What did I just say?' and one shy little girl very quietly repeated my words back to me. I was quick to correct it.

Needless to say, my daughter informed me that she would NOT be coming to "Take Your Daughter to Work Day" that year.

TEACHERS.NET/CHATBOARD

While taking a routine vandalism report at an elementary school, I was interrupted by a little girl about six years old. Looking up and down at my uniform, she asked, "Are you a cop?"

"Yes," I answered and continued writing the report.

"My mother said if I ever needed help I should ask the police. Is that right?"

"Yes, that's right," I told her.

"Well, then," she said as she extended her foot toward me, "would you please tie my shoe?"

BECQUET.COM

In my class, when a person has a birthday, instead of being given a present, the birthday person brings a book to our class for the in-room library. On my birthday, I chose my favorite book: *There's a Boy in the Girls' Bathroom*.

I went to the bookstore and asked the lady behind the counter, "Do you carry *There's a Boy in the Girls' Bathroom*?" Instead of looking it up on the computer as I thought she would, she said, "Just a minute," and she disappeared. My mom and I waited and waited.

Finally she came back, and she said to me, "There's no one there now—he must have gone home with his mother."

MELANIE HANSEN, AGE 10

A little girl who was attending a progressive school had a cold one morning and her mother suggested that she remain home from school. "But I can't, Mother," the child insisted, "this is the day when we start to make a clay model of a cow and I'm chairman of the udder committee."

EDMUND FULLER, *2500 ANECDOTES FOR ALL OCCASIONS*

I often use phrases my students don't understand. To me they are common sayings, but not to this generation. Having drawn some really horrible facsimiles of polyhedrons on the board, I apologized for the poor artwork and told them that my artwork was "from hunger."

Immediately one kid asked if I was from Hungary, and another corrected him and said, "No stupid, she said she's hungry."

TEACHERS.NET/CHATBOARD

LETTER PERFECT

Alfred, you're reading much better!
Alfred, your homework's complete!
Alfred, you've learned to write cursive!
Alfred, you've learned to be neat!

Alfred, your grade's sixty-nine now.
Alfred, you're . . . well, I'll be blunt:
Alfred, a seventy's passing.
Alfred, I'm sorry; you flunk.

CHERYL MILLER THURSTON

Here's what really bugs me:
Teachers who give assignments like WHAT I DID ON MY SUMMER VACATION.

What if you didn't have a vacation? What if you had a lemonade stand and worked all summer and what if you only made four bucks and some change and the lemons and sugar and cardboard for the stand cost much more than you made. Plus $2.60 for a broken punch bowl. Would I want to write about this horrible experience? I don't think so.

JANE WAGNER

The day of a big snowstorm, the country school teacher felt called upon to warn her charges against playing too long in the snow. She said, "Now, children, you must be careful about colds and over-exposure. I had a darling little brother only seven years old. One day he went out in the snow with his new sled and caught cold. Pneumonia set in and three days later he died."

The room was silent and then a youngster in the back row raised his hand and asked, "Where's his sled?"

EDMUND FULLER, *2500 ANECDOTES FOR ALL OCCASIONS*

Since children say what they think in a straightforward way, nothing means more to a teacher than a child's compliment. So you can imagine the warm glow Mrs. Hudson felt when a little girl slipped her hand shyly into hers and said, "Mrs. Hudson, do you know who is the prettiest teacher in the school?"

"No. Who is?"

"Miss Wilson."

BECQUET.COM

To be a first-grade teacher you have to have skill, dedication, and an immunity to knock-knock jokes.

ANONYMOUS

Ms. Tamberg asked her Monday morning first-grade class, "What did you do for fun this weekend?"

Melody spoke up, "I went to the zoo with my mama and daddy."

"Really?" her teacher said. "Did your brothers and sister go with you?"

"No, ma'am," Melody answered. "I don't have any brothers and sisters. In fact, my mama can't have any more children . . . she had her tonsils out!"

JUDY MOON DENSON AND BEVERLY SMALLWOOD, *KIDSPIRATION*

I was student teaching in first grade, and we had just begun subtraction. One day I started a math lesson by asking for a word that starts with an "s" and means "taking away." One girl raised her hand and answered, "Stealing."

VERONICA ENNS ON TEACHERNET.COM

The lesson in natural history had been about the rhinoceros, and I was following it with an oral test.

"Now, name something," I said, "that is very dangerous to get near to, and that has horns."

"I know, Miss Lane, I know!" called little Jennie.

"Well, Jennie, what is it?" I asked.

"An automobile!" Jennie replied triumphantly.

RITA LANE IN *KID STUFF*

My mom is a first-grade teacher. It was around Christmas, and all the kids were really hyper. A little boy came into her room and put a coffee mug filled with toy soldiers on her desk. She asked what it was for, and he said, "The best part of waking up is soldiers in your cup."

VANESSA BREEDEN, AGE 12

I had just returned from taking my first grade students to the bathroom. I introduced my next lesson and everyone was working diligently when Bobby approached my desk.

"May I go to the bathroom?"

"But, Bobby, we just got back from the bathroom."

"Yes teacher, I know. But that time I had to stand up. This time I have to sit down."

JOAN CLAYTON

Judith Frost Stark, a first grade school teacher, gave her students the beginning of cliches and then asked them to finish the thought. Here is a sampling of what they wrote:

- People who live in glass houses shouldn't . . . undress.
- If you lie down with the dogs . . . you'll stink in the morning.
- When the cat's away . . . no pooh!
- A penny saved is . . . not much.
- Opportunity only knocks when . . . she can't reach the doorbell.

JUDITH FROST STARK

The first-grader was talking about the recent fire in his school. "I knew it was going to happen," he said. "We had been practicing for it all year."

HARRY B. OTIS

In preparing her second-graders for a critical standardized test, Linda, [a second grade teacher], stressed the importance of listening and following all her directions.

The children began working, and as she casually strolled around she noticed Bobby working frantically over his paper. She was horrified to see he'd covered his test with huge check marks made with a bright red crayon.

"Bobby, what have you done?!" she gasped. "You've ruined your test!"

"No, ma'am." He calmly shook his head. "You told us to check every answer so I did!"

LIZ CURTIS HIGGS

As a second grade teacher in Sunnyvale, California, I am fortunate to have lovely weather and to have my school near the monarch butterfly migrating path. We have a garden of milkweed to attract these lovely butterflies. This year we were able to actually see a butterfly lay eggs on a leaf and brought it into the classroom to watch the entire cycle of metamorphosis take place. One of my [English as a] second language students was very excited to tell our new fourth grade male teacher that this teacher could come to our classroom and watch the butterflies go through menopause.

TERRY YORDAN

Typically, it's not until third grade that students learn how to write in cursive. That fact saved "face" for Curtis—a boy in my second grade class. We were coming back on a bus from a field trip. The kids on it ranged in grades from first through sixth. One of the kids began teasing Curtis, saying he'd written a love note to a girl. The teasing went on until Curtis couldn't take it anymore. He swung around and demanded, "Was it in cur-shuf?" When the other boy shook his head indicating that it was, Curtis settled back with a smile on his face.

PATRICIA HARRINGTON

Miss Mayfield had been giving her second-grade students a lesson on science. She had explained about magnets and showed how they could pick up nails and other bits of iron. Now it was question time, and she asked, "My name begins with the letter 'M' and I pick things up. What am I?"

A little boy in the front row said, "You're a mother."

RICHARD LEDERER

My favorite classroom story concerns a young third-grade girl who came to school one morning all excited. She explained that things were really different at their house now because her grandfather had come to live with them. Then, she said: "And he's sterile, you know."

The teacher thought for a moment and then replied: "You mean senile, don't you?"

The child replied: "That, too!"

WARNING! CUTE KID STORIES AHEAD!

The last part of the third-graders' test required them to find four mistakes in a paragraph that talked about Helen Keller and mentioned the movie *The Miracle Worker*.

Zech had found three of the mistakes and was desperately searching for the fourth.

Finally, the title *"The Miracle Worker"* caught his eye. "I know," he shouted triumphantly. "It should be Miracle Whip!"

GRACE WITWER HOUSHOLDER

My third-grader Cindy came dashing in from the school bus. "I mustn't forget to take a quarter to school tomorrow!" she exclaimed excitedly.

When I asked why, she said, "Oh, it's important. Our teacher is leaving and all the kids want to give her a little momentum!"

ROBERTA RICH IN *KID STUFF*

A teacher says to her third grade class, "Children, I'm going to ask each of you what your father does for a living. Bobby, you'll go first."

So Bobby stands up and says, "My father runs the bank."

The teacher says, "Thank you," and calls on Sarah.

Sarah stands up and tells the teacher, "My father is a chef."

Again, the teacher says, "Thank you," and calls on Joey.

So Joey stands up and says, "My father is a politician and took bribes in the pub over in Queens."

So the teacher becomes very upset and changes the subject to arithmetic.

Later that day, after school, the teacher goes to Joey's house and knocks on the door.

And Joey's father answers it and says, "Yes? Can I help you?"

And the teacher says, "Your son Joey is in my third grade class. What is this I hear about you being in the pub bribery scandal in Queens?"

And the father says, "You see, actually, I'm an attorney. But you try telling that to an eight-year-old kid!"

SOUPY SALES

chalk´ board n. — the thing the teacher faces
to allow you to fool around.

RICK DETORIE

The third grade teacher asked one of her students to go to the blackboard to write a sentence. When the young boy got to the blackboard he turned to the teacher and said, "I ain't got no chalk."

"That is not correct," said the teacher. "The right way is, I don't have any chalk; you don't have any chalk; we don't have any chalk; they don't have any chalk. Now, do you understand?"

"No," said the boy. "What happened to all the chalk?"

ANONYMOUS

A fourth grader had the sniffles and it annoyed the teacher so bad that she finally asked him, "Do you have a handkerchief?"

He said, "Yea, but my mom won't let me loan it to anyone."

RON DENTINGER

A fifth grade teacher was teaching a lesson in logic. "Here is the situation," she said. "A man is standing up in a boat in the middle of a river. Suddenly, he loses his balance and falls in. He begins splashing around in the strong current and yelling for help. His wife hears the commotion, knows he can't swim, and runs down to the riverbank. Why do you think she ran to the bank?"

A girl raised her hand and replied, "To draw out all his savings!"

ANONYMOUS

During a lesson in first aid, one teacher asked what is the name of the procedure used to help someone who is choking? The correct answer would have been "Heimlich maneuver." But one young student, who thought she knew the answer, raised her hand and innocently replied, "It is called the Hymen Remover."

ANONYMOUS

78

The fifth-grader had been only partially attentive to the discussion about Greece. The teacher followed through with a question, "What do you know about Socrates?"

"Oh," blurted the child like a deer caught in headlights, "I know, I know. Didn't he invent that . . . maneuver?"

The teacher looked confused. "Maneuver?"

"Yeah," the student continued. "That move doctors use when people choke. You know—the hemlock maneuver."

PAUL KARRER

When you're in the fifth grade and faced with having to choose between eternal life and recess, eternal life doesn't stand a chance.

TONY VANARIA

The teacher asked each member of her sixth-grade class to write the names of nine outstanding Americans. Ten minutes later, the teacher saw that everyone but Carl had finished writing.

"What's the matter, Carl?" the teacher said. "Can't you think of nine great Americans?"

"I have eight," Carl said. "But I still need a second baseman."

THE RANDOM HOUSE BOOK OF JOKES AND ANECDOTES

Sixth-graders in Oklahoma
are using worms to recycle garbage
from school lunches. But even the worms
won't eat the macaroni and cheese.

ANONYMOUS

Junior High and High School

The hardest job I had was substitute teaching in junior high. An eighth-grade boy got mad over a math assignment I gave him and went all over school telling everyone that I was a centerfold in *Playboy* magazine. I was fuming mad. At recess, two regular teachers sidled up to me in the coffee room and wanted to know if what they heard . . . was, uh, true. All at once I found myself putting the pain in perspective as I responded, "It is a mean, nasty lie, and I certainly hope no one gets ahold of August of '61."

Virginia Tooper

A brand new English teacher in a small northern New Hampshire junior high school assigned her class the reading of *The Swiss Family Robinson*. This children's classic is about the adventures of a family marooned on a desert island. During the course of the story a large boa constrictor wraps itself around the family's donkey and devours the entire animal.

Here's how one of the seventh-graders described the incident: "The snake crept up, opened its jaws wide, and swallowed the ass whole."

Richard Lederer

The local fire chief had worked out an orderly plan for a speedy evacuation of the local junior high school in case of fire. After several practice fire drills, the chief told the principal, "One more time. This is it. This time we'll hold a stop watch on the kids to see how well they do."

Bells rang, kids lined up and marched according to the chief's plan, and nobody made a mistake or lost a moment's time. Perfect. No confusion. The schoolhouse was empty.

Time: three minutes, sixteen seconds.

Fifteen minutes later it was time for recess. The bells rang. The kids scrambled. And soon the schoolhouse was again empty.

Time: two minutes, three seconds.

WINSTON K. PENDLETON, *COMPLETE SPEAKER'S GALAXY OF FUNNY STORIES, JOKES AND ANECDOTES*

Waves of students are surging in and out of the high school's main office, trying to find out which rooms they're supposed to go to. This is determined by a complex schedule apparently designed so that, whenever the bell rings, every student in the school has to bump into every other student to get to the next class.

DAVE BARRY

A high-school student was called on to make a brief unprepared speech on Lincoln. Mindful of his teacher's advice that frequently it is possible to make a reasonably good talk by building on the preceding sentence, the student confidently and solemnly began with "Lincoln is dead." After waiting, in vain, for another thought to be suggested by this statement, he again said "Lincoln is dead." Once more he declared "Lincoln is dead"—and added, in desperation, "and I don't feel so good myself either."

HYMAN ALPERN

82

History According to Student Bloopers:

- Early Egyptian women often wore a garment called a calasiris. It was a sheer dress which started beneath the breasts which hung to the floor.

- The Greeks invented three kinds of columns—corynthian, ironic, and dorc.

- Life during the Middle Ages was especially difficult for the pheasants.

- Sir Francis Drake circumcised the world with a 100-foot clipper.

RICHARD LEDERER

A teacher in a first-aid class received the following letter from a former student:

I want to thank you for the wonderful training you gave me in first aid. I am lucky I remembered yesterday what you taught us so long ago. I was crossing the street when I heard a crash. I turned around and there was a poor man lying there—struck down by a truck. It looked like he had a broken leg and he was bleeding profusely. Then all my first aid came back to me. I stooped down and put my head between my knees to keep from fainting.

ANONYMOUS

83

A high school in Connecticut has a
power-nap club. We called that algebra class.

JAY LENO

Silly Similes from High School Essays:

- Her vocabulary was as bad as, like, whatever.
- The little boat gently drifted across the pond exactly the way a bowling ball wouldn't.
- He was as lame as a duck. Not the metaphorical lame duck, either, but a real duck that was actually lame. Maybe from stepping on a land mine or something.
- The ballerina rose gracefully en pointe and extended one slender leg behind her, like a dog at a fire hydrant.
- He was deeply in love. When she spoke, he thought he heard bells, as if she were a garbage truck backing up.

ANONYMOUS

Young scholars around our nation manage to mangle the mother tongue with bizarre word choices:

- In the United States, criminals are put to death by elocution.
- The police called 911 to get an ambulance to take him to the mortgage.
- In Venice the people travel around the canals on gorgonzolas.
- During the 1920's, several films were released in two virgins: one silent and the other with sounds.
- A census taker is a man who goes from house to house increasing the population.

RICHARD LEDERER

One beautiful spring morning, three high school seniors played hooky from their class. After lunch, the boys returned to school and told the teacher that they had a flat tire while driving to school. The teacher smiled and said, "Boys, you missed a test this morning. Take a seat apart from one another and get out a blank sheet of paper."

"Here is your first question," the teacher said. "Which tire was flat?"

ANONYMOUS

TESTING, TESTING, TESTING!

Testing, Testing, Testing!
They're testing us to death.
At school, we take so many tests
we're almost out of breath . . .

From testing, testing, testing!
It's all we seem to do.
If you could look inside our brains,
you'd see they're black-and-blue . . .

From testing, testing, testing!
And that is my concern.
We take so many tests each week
there's never time to learn.

TED SCHEU

Just before Christmas, a teacher was examining the tests handed in by her high school class. On one it said: "God only knows the answer to this question. Merry Christmas!" The teacher wrote across this paper: "God gets an 'A.' You get an 'F.' Happy New Year!"

ANONYMOUS

College

ACADEME, n. An ancient school where morality and philosophy were taught.

ACADEMY, n. (from academe). A modern school where football is taught.

AMBROSE BIERCE

My son is a senior in high school, which means that pretty soon he'll probably select a college. We've already gone on several college visits. Most college visits include an orientation session, wherein you sit in a lecture room and a college official tells you impressive statistics about the college, including, almost always, how small the classes are. Class smallness is considered the ultimate measure of how good a college is. Harvard, for example, has zero students per class: The professors just sit alone in their classrooms, filing their nails.

DAVE BARRY

When I first started college, the dean came in and said "Good Morning" to all of us. When we echoed back to him, he responded "Ah, you're freshmen."

"He explained, "When you walk in and say "good morning," and they say "good morning" back, it's freshmen.

"When they put their newspapers down and open their books, it's sophomores.

"When they look up so they can see the instructor over the tops of the newspapers, it's juniors.

"When they put their feet up on the desks and keep reading, it's seniors.

"When you walk in and say "good morning" and they write it down, it's graduate students."

ANONYMOUS

On the first day of college, the dean addressed the new students explaining some of the campus rules:

"The female dormitory will be out-of-bounds for all male students, and the male dormitory out-of-bounds to the female students. Anybody caught breaking this rule will be fined $50 the first time. Anybody caught breaking this rule the second time will be fined $100. Being caught a third time will cost $200. Are there any questions?"

One student yelled out, "How much for a season pass?"

ANONYMOUS

Fun Things for Professors to Do on the First Day of Class

- After confirming everyone's names on the roll, thank the class for attending "Advanced Astrodynamics 690" and mention that yesterday was the last day to drop.

- Announce "You'll need this," and write the suicide prevention hotline number on the board.

- Wear mirrored sunglasses and speak only in Turkish. Ignore all questions.

- Ask the class to read "Jenkins" through "Johnson" of the local phone book by the next lecture. Vaguely imply that there will be a quiz.

- Mention in passing that you're wearing rubber underwear.

ANONYMOUS

We have a daughter who's two months into her freshman year. Judging from her phone calls, I think she's majoring in Panic.

And the courses she's taking. One is called "An Introduction to the Cinema." For those of you not familiar with "An Introduction to the Cinema"—it's when your kids pay a hundred dollars a point to see the same movies you saw at twenty-five cents on Saturday night.... they get a degree and you got dishes.

ROBERT ORBEN, *2400 JOKES TO BRIGHTEN YOUR SPEECHES*

College is the best time of your life. When else are your parents going to spend several thousand dollars a year just for you to go to a strange town and get drunk every night?

DAVID WOOD

A chain-smoking college boy declared one day: "I have been reading so very much about how bad smoking is for you, that I have made a drastic decision—I've given up reading."

ANONYMOUS

The professor of an economics class asks, "If all the advertising for food products were to stop tomorrow, how many people would stop eating?"

A guy in the back says, "A whole bunch of advertising executives."

RON DENTINGER

College professor—someone who talks in other people's sleep.

BERGEN EVANS

Professors must have a theory as a dog must have fleas.

WILLIAM J. BRYAN

Students enrolled in a Russian language course at Eckerd College approached their first class with some apprehension about its difficulty. The professor entered the room, followed by his dog. Before saying a word to the students, he commanded the dog to sit, beg, lie down, roll over—all in Russian. The dog obeyed each command perfectly.

"See how easy Russian is," the professor said. "Why, even a dog can learn it!"

STEVE ALLEN, *STEVE ALLEN'S PRIVATE JOKE FILE*

A professor put the following bonus question in a test to his psychology students: "What sign was posted on the door of Pavlov's famous institute?"

After the test, the students discussed this but could not come up with a consensus of what the correct answer might be. So one student went to the professor's office to ask him.

Without cracking a smile, the professor replied, "Please knock. Don't ring bell."

ANONYMOUS

In college, Yuppies major in business administration.
If to meet certain requirements they have to take
a liberal arts course, they take Business Poetry.

DAVE BARRY

When a subject becomes totally obsolete
we make it a required course.

PETER DRUCKER

A professor was grading the essay finals he had just given his class and opened the exam book of a failing student to reveal blank pages and a $100 bill. The only thing written in the book was "$100 = 100% —I get an A."

A month later, the student approached the professor. "I don't understand," he said. "I failed the course. Didn't you read my final?" The professor handed the student the exam book.

The student opened it to reveal $50 and the phrase "$50 = 50% —You fail!"

ANONYMOUS

A lecture is an occasion when you numb one end
to benefit the other.

JOHN GOULD

A speaker was booked to address an audience at a university. About two hours before she was supposed to speak, however, a couple of student jokers loaded a truck with all of the folding chairs in the auditorium and drove off. No one knew about this until the audience began to arrive for the lecture. It was too late to do anything about it, and the audience had to stand throughout her talk. That evening she wrote a letter to her mother: "It was a tremendous success. Hours before I got there, every seat in the house was taken, and I was given a standing ovation throughout my speech."

ILANA WEITZMAN, EVA BLANK, AND ROSEANNE GREEN, *JOKELOPEDIA*

It is possible for a student to win twelve letters at a university without his learning how to write one.

ROBERT MAYNARD HUTCHINS

I was teaching a course in Advanced Abnormal Psychology with the special title of "Exotic Syndromes". Thus, some of the material was pretty racy, relative to the usual run of abnormalities. I was lecturing on the intricacies of "S & M". One studious young lady asked me, "How do you spell that?"

LOU FRANZINI

It was the final examination for an introductory English course at the local university. Like many such freshman courses, it was designed to weed out new students, having over 700 students in the class! The examination was two hours long, and exam booklets were provided. The professor was very strict and told the class that any exam that was not on his desk in exactly two hours would not be accepted and the student would fail. A half-hour into the exam, a student came rushing in and asked the professor for an exam booklet. "You're not going to have time to finish this," the professor stated sarcastically as he handed the student a booklet.

"Yes I will," replied the student. He then took a seat and began writing.

After two hours, the professor called for the exams, and the students filed up and handed them in. All except the late student, who continued writing. A half-hour later, the last student came up to the professor who was sitting at his desk preparing for his next class. He attempted to put his exam on the stack of exam booklets already there.

"No you don't, I'm not going to accept that. It's late."

The student looked incredulous and angry. "Do you know WHO I am?"

"No, as a matter of fact I don't," replied the professor with an air of sarcasm in his voice.

"DO YOU KNOW WHO I AM?" the student asked again.

"No, and I don't care," replied the professor with an air of superiority.

"Good," replied the student, who quickly lifted the stack of completed exams, stuffed his in the middle, and walked out of the room.

ANONYMOUS

Comments from the MIT Course Evaluation Guide, Fall 1991

- "The recitation instructor would make a good parking lot attendant. Tries to tell you where to go, but you can never understand him."

- "Recitation was great. It was so confusing that I forgot who I was, where I was, and what I was doing—it's a great stress reliever."

- "TA steadily improved throughout the course...I think he started drinking and it really loosened him up."

- "What's the quality of the text? 'Text is printed on high quality paper.'"

- "Text is useless. I use it to kill roaches in my room."

Intelligence is when you spot a flaw in your teacher's reasoning. Wisdom is when you refrain from pointing it out.

JAMES DENT

Miss Katharine Cater served as Dean of Women at Auburn University for, well, it seemed like forever. Generations of Auburn women both respected this outstanding woman and, quite honestly, feared her in a nice sort of way. She practically ruled the lives of those of us who attended college when young women still checked in and out of the dorm according to certain hours. If we missed a curfew, we were restricted to our rooms. Few explanations were accepted. One can understand, therefore, how quickly the next occurrence spread around the campus.

During the sixties, the officers of the Women's Student Government Association and Dean Cater attended a meeting in Birmingham and, lo and behold, had a flat tire on the way back to Auburn. While they stood on the side of the highway trying to decide what to do, one of the students (surely a graduating senior) couldn't resist a comment. "You see, Dean Cater. You can too have a flat tire on the way back to the dorm."

JEANNE ROBERTSON

I find that the three major administrative problems
on a campus are sex for the students, athletics for
the alumni, and parking for the faculty.

CLARK KERR

Mr. Paley, the biology instructor at a posh suburban girl's junior college, said during class, "Miss Thompson, would you please name the organ of the human body, which under the appropriate conditions, expands to six times its normal size, and define the conditions."

Miss Thompson gasped, then said, "Mr. Paley, I don't think that is a proper question to ask me. I assure you my parents will hear of this." With that she sat down red-faced.

Unperturbed, Mr. Paley called on Miss Simpson and asked the same question. Miss Simpson, with composure, replied, "The pupil of the eye, in dim light."

"Correct," said Mr. Paley.

"And now, Miss Thompson, I have three things to say to you. One, you have not studied your lesson. Two, you have a dirty mind. And three, you will someday be faced with a dreadful disappointment."

ANONYMOUS

SHOW AND TELL

HOMEWORK

PARENT-TEACHER MATTERS

A+

REPORT CARDS

WHEN I WENT TO SCHOOL

The three most frightening words a student could hear were: "Bring Your Mother." It was the equivalent of a death warrant. You pleaded, you cried, you invented heartrending excuses. "My mother can't come. She's sick, she can't climb stairs, she's dying, I'm an orphan, I live all by myself. Bring my father? He died four years before I was born, he can't come, he works in Alaska, he comes home only on Saturdays. What did I do? Tell me! I'll never do it again. I never did it before so I'll never do it again."

SAM LEVENSON

Sam Levenson was especially interested in the relationship between children and their parents, especially the matter of child psychology and its popular distortions. "One mother," he recalled "wrote a note to the teacher. If Gregory is a bad boy, she says, don't slap him. Slap the boy *next* to him. Gregory will get the idea."

WILLIAM NOVAK AND MOSHE WALDOKS

Teacher conference: A meeting between Mom and that person who has yet to understand her child's "special needs."

ANONYMOUS

PARENT-TEACHER CONFERENCE

My homework's always overdue—
it makes my teacher mad.
So, she arranged a meeting with
my mother and my dad.

I know she wants to ask them both
why I procrastinate.
But she may never get the chance—
my parents both are late.

TED SCHEU

Teacher: Mrs. Jones, I asked you to come in to discuss Johnny's appearance.

Mrs Jones: Why? What's wrong with his appearance?

Teacher: He hasn't made one in this classroom since September.

ILANA WEITZMAN, EVA BLANK, AND ROSEANNE GREEN, *JOKELOPEDIA*

Teacher's truism: The only time parents are willing to accept their child as "average" is at the moment of birth.

ANONYMOUS

Note from parent: "Please excuse Bobby for not having his homework today, he didn't have a pencil at home." Note written in PENCIL.

TEACHERSZINE.COM

Voice over telephone: Henry Watkins will not be in school today. He is sick in bed with the flu.

School Secretary: And who is speaking?

Voice: My father.

ANONYMOUS

Excuses, Excuses:

- Mary could not come to school because she has been bothered by very close veins.
- Please excuse Ray Friday from school. He has very loose vowels.
- Please excuse Mary for being absent, yesterday. She was in bed with gramps.
- Gloria was absent yesterday as she was having a gangover.
- Please excuse Burma, she has been sick and under the doctor.

RICHARD LEDERER

**Please excuse Harold for not having his homework.
His Internet service provider's servers were down and he
couldn't connect to his online homework helpline.**

AARON BACALL

**Teacher to parent: "Not only is your son the worst behaved
child in my class, but he has perfect attendance."**

ANONYMOUS

103

Teacher: Well, at least there's one thing I can say about your son.

Father: What's that?

Teacher: With grades like these, he couldn't be cheating.

JOSEPH ROSENBLOOM, *696 SILLY SCHOOL JOKES & RIDDLES*

**Schoolteachers are not fully appreciated by parents until it rains
all day Saturday.**

E. C. MCKENZIE, *14,000 QUIPS AND QUOTES FOR WRITERS AND SPEAKERS*

"PTA" means different things to different people.
If you're a parent, it means Parents Threatening Action.
If you're a school administrator, it means
Principals Taking Aspirin.

ROBERT ORBEN, *2500 JOKES TO START 'EM LAUGHING*

SHOW AND TELL

Then there is the teacher who, on the first day of school, sends each of her students home with the following note:

We start Show and Tell tomorrow. If you promise not to believe everything your child says happens in class, I promise not to believe everything he says happens at home.

SAM LEVENSON

I'd like to say a few words about one of the most popular concepts in modern education—show and tell. Show and tell is a device created by grammar schools to communicate family secrets to thirty-two other families before 9:15 in the morning!

ROBERT ORBEN

The big game hunter was telling about his adventures to a group of school children during their show-and-tell period. In describing some of his exciting experiences in Africa he said, "One night I remember being wakened by a great roaring noise. I jumped up and grabbed my gun, which I always kept loaded at the foot of my cot. I rushed out and killed a huge lion in my pajamas."

At the close of his presentation he asked if there were any questions.

"Yes," said a little girl sitting in the front row, "how did the lion get into your pajamas?"

WINSTON K. PENDLETON, *COMPLETE SPEAKER'S GALAXY OF FUNNY STORIES, JOKES AND ANECDOTES*

One day this little girl, Erica, a very bright, very outgoing kid, takes her turn [at show and tell] and waddles up to the front of the class with a pillow stuffed under her sweater. She holds up a snapshot of an infant. "This is Luke, my baby brother, and I'm going to tell you about his birthday. First, Mom and Dad made him as a symbol of their love, and then Dad put a seed in my Mom's stomach, and Luke grew in there. He ate for nine months through an umbrella cord."

She's standing there with her hands on the pillow, and I'm trying not to laugh and wishing I had my camcorder with me. The kids are watching her in amazement. "Then, about two Saturdays ago, my Mom starts saying and going, 'Oh, oh, oh, oh!'" (Erica puts a hand behind her back and groans.) "She walked around the house for, like an hour, 'Oh, oh, oh!'" (Now this kid is doing a hysterical duck walk and groaning.)

"My Dad called the middle wife. She delivers babies, but she doesn't have a sign on the car like the Domino's man. They got my Mom to lie down in bed like this." (Then Erica lies down with her back against the wall.) "And then, pop! My Mom had this bag of water she kept in there in case he got thirsty, and it just blew up and spilled all over the bed, like psshhheew!" . . .

"Then the middle wife starts saying 'push, push,' and 'breathe, breathe.' They started counting, but never even got past ten. Then, all of a sudden, out comes my brother. He was covered in yucky stuff. They all said it was from Mom's play-center, so there must be a lot of stuff inside there."

Then Erica stood up, took a big theatrical bow and returned to her seat.

ANONYMOUS

Homework

home´ work n. —something for which there are
6,874 reasons to forget to bring it to school.

RICK DETORIE

Students should not spend more than ninety minutes each night on homework. The time should be budgeted in the following manner:

Time	*Task*
15 minutes	Looking for assignment.
11 minutes	Calling a friend for the assignment.
23 minutes	Explaining why the teacher is mean and just does not like children.
8 minutes	Going to the bathroom.
10 minutes	Getting a snack.
7 minutes	Checking the *TV Guide*.
6 minutes	Telling parents that the teacher never explained the assignment.
10 minutes	Waiting for Mom or Dad to do the assignment.

ANONYMOUS

I was teaching a science lesson on the different forms of life. The homework assignment was to write a one-page paper on different types of organisms. The following day I was amazed and amused when one young lady turned in her homework assignment titled, "The Screaming Orgasm."

Anonymous

Top 10 Excuses for Unfinished Homework:

10. My dog ate it.

9. My cat used it in her litter box.

8. My little sister flushed it down the toilet as a science experiment.

7. It burned, along with my house.

6. It fell in the mud and you can't read it.

5. That bully beat me up on the playground and took it.

4. The wind blew it out of my hand and now it's "Gone With the Wind."

3. We were robbed last night. They didn't get the VCR, but they did take my homework.

2. My Dad accidentally used it to start a fire in our fireplace.

1. What? What homework? I didn't hear you assign anything!

Richard A. Shade

Teacher: Johnny, where is your homework?

Johnny: I lost it fighting with a boy who said that you weren't the best teacher in the whole school.

ANONYMOUS

Don't tell a teacher your dog ate your homework, especially if you don't have a dog.

RAELYN RITCHIE, AGE 12

The reason you want your kids to pay attention in school is that you haven't the faintest idea how to do their homework.

BABS BELL HAJDUSIEWICZ

The toughest thing about homework is getting mom and pop to agree on the same answer.

JOEY ADAMS

A little girl came home from school and said to her mother, "Mommy, today in school I was punished for something that I didn't do."

The mother exclaimed, "But that's terrible! I'm going to have a talk with your teacher about this—by the way, what was it that you didn't do?"

The little girl replied, "My homework."

ANONYMOUS

Top Ten Excuses for Submitting a Late Homework Assignment:

10. I thought Groundhog Day was a national holiday.

9. My pit bull ate my ferret, which ate my homework.

8. After watching *Oprah*, I realized that homework lowers my self-esteem.

7. I was too wrapped up in the latest *Survivor* episode.

6. I think I'm ADD.

5. My assignment was confiscated by Homeland Security officials.

4. The answers for the assignment were not in the *CliffsNotes*.

3. My mom didn't have the time to complete my homework.

2. I accidentally drank a six-pack of beer and thought I had already graduated.

1. Hey, President Bush was a C student.

MEL HELITZER

Report Cards

Report card: A piece of paper that lets you realize you
don't have to be a weight lifter to raise a dumbbell.

ANONYMOUS

Suggested Comments on Report Cards:

- This young lady has delusions of adequacy.
- This student should go far, and the sooner he starts, the better.
- Got a full 6-pack, but lacks the plastic thing to hold it together.
- He doesn't have ulcers, but he's a carrier.
- He's been working with glue too much.
- When his I.Q. reaches 50, he should sell.
- A photographic memory but with the lens cover glued on.
- Gates are down, the lights are flashing, but the train isn't coming.
- If you give him a penny for his thoughts, you'd get change.
- Takes him 1 1/2 hours to watch 60 minutes.

ANONYMOUS

When I came home and showed my mother my report
card with a mark of 98 in arithmetic, she wanted to know
who had gotten the other two points.

SAM LEVENSON

A young school boy wasn't getting very good grades. One day he
surprised the teacher when he tapped her on the shoulder and
said, "I don't want to scare you, but my daddy says if I don't get
good grades on my report card someone will get a spanking!"

ANONYMOUS

One January, a young man came home from school with an
unsatisfactory report card. After reviewing the bad report,
his mother wanted to know what was wrong.

"There isn't anything wrong," said the youngster. "You know
how it is; things are always marked down after the holidays."

ANONYMOUS

WHEN I WENT TO SCHOOL

In kindergarten, I flunked sandpile.
JOEY BISHOP

I was coming home from kindergarten—well, they told me it was kindergarten. I found out later I had been working in a factory for ten years. It's good for a kid to know how to make gloves.
ELLEN DEGENERES

I will never forget my first day of school. My mom woke me up, got me dressed, made my bed, and fed me. Man, did the guys in the dorm tease me.
MICHAEL ARONIN

Smartness runs in the family. When I went to school
I was so smart my teacher was in my class for five years.

GRACIE ALLEN

In the sixth grade they wanted me to
count up to ten—from memory.

HENNY YOUNGMAN

I once played hooky from school.
My teacher sent a thank-you note!

MILTON BERLE, *MILTON BERLE'S PRIVATE JOKE FILE*

My first grade school teacher said,
"Okay, Mark, tell us everything you know about
the letter H." I said, "That's Jesus' middle name."

MARK LUNDHOLM

I always did well on essay questions. Just put everything you
know in there, maybe you'll hit it. And you'll always get it back
from the teacher, and she's just written one word across the entire
page, "Vague." I thought "vague" was kind of a vague thing to say.
I'd write underneath it, "Unclear," send it back. She'd return it to
me, "Ambiguous." I'd send it back to her, "Cloudy." We're still
corresponding to this day— "Hazy"; "Muddy."

JERRY SEINFELD

In first grade my teacher asked what I expected of life.
I said, "You color for a while, then you die."

JEFFREY ESSMANN

I was always getting into trouble in school and it
wasn't my fault. One time I raised my hand and said,
"Can I go to the bathroom?" The teacher said, "Did I hear
you say 'can'?" I said, "No, I said 'bathroom.'"

ROBERT ORBEN, *2500 JOKES TO START 'EM LAUGHING*

I had a terrible time when I was eleven years old.
First, I got tonsillitis, which was followed by pneumonia. Then
I got appendicitis and that was followed by poliomyelitis. After
that I got catarrh and finally ended up with bronchitis. Then they
gave me analgesics and inoculations.
I honestly can't remember having a worse spelling test.

THE PENGUIN DICTIONARY OF JOKES

I quit school in the fifth grade because of pneumonia.
Not because I had it but because I couldn't spell it

ROCKY GRAZIANO

I had a terrible education. I attended a school
for emotionally disturbed teachers.

WOODY ALLEN

I will never forget my school days. I was teacher's pet.
She couldn't afford a dog.

HENNY YOUNGMAN

When I was in school, one of my teachers was crazy
about me. I once heard her tell another teacher,
"I wish he was my kid for one day!"

MILTON BERLE, *MILTON BERLE'S PRIVATE JOKE FILE*

I read Shakespeare and the Bible and I can shoot dice.
That's what I call a liberal education.

TALLULAH BANKHEAD (ATTRIBUTED)

I can remember when I was a kid we used to write the answers
to questions on our fingernails. One time I got so nervous,
I chewed up two years of Intermediate Algebra!

ROBERT ORBEN, *2400 JOKES TO BRIGHTEN YOUR SPEECHES*

Stand firm in your refusal to remain conscious during algebra.
In real life, I assure you, there is no such thing as algebra.

FRAN LEBOWITZ

It's strange how few of the world's great problems are
solved by people who remember their algebra.

HERBERT PROCHNOW

My school motto was *'Monsanto incorpori glorius mexima copia'* which in Latin means, "When the going gets tough, the tough go shopping."

ROBIN WILLIAMS

In high school, I was voted the girl most likely to become a nun. That may not be impressive to you, but it was quite an accomplishment at the Hebrew Academy.

RITA RUDNER

I was thrown out of college for cheating on the metaphysics exam; I looked into the soul of the boy next to me.

WOODY ALLEN

In elementary school during Student Government Week, I was Coroner for the Day.

RICHARD LEWIS

I studied the Constitution in high school, learned the Fourth Amendment. That's the one concerned with search and seizure. For example, if my mother had searched my room, she would've had a seizure.

NORMAN K.

When I finished school I took one of those career aptitude tests and, based on my verbal ability score, they suggested I become a mime.

TIM CAVANAUGH

Old teachers never die, they just grade away.
ANONYMOUS

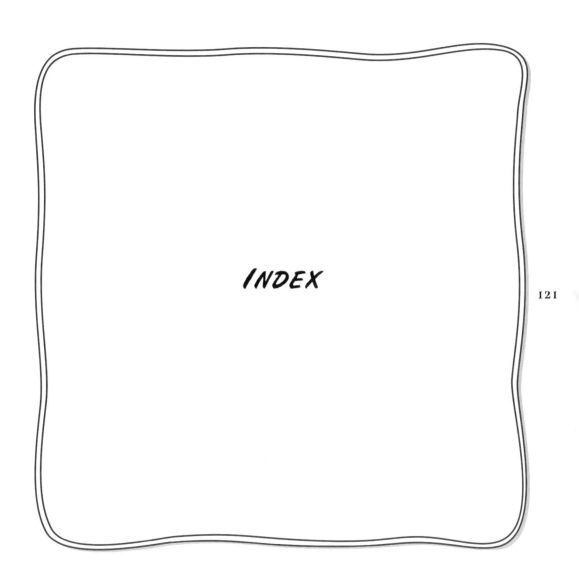

INDEX

696 Silly School Jokes & Riddles 26, 31, 44, 63, 103

2400 Jokes to Brighten Your Speeches 16, 89, 117

2500 Anecdotes for All Occasions 68, 70

2500 Jokes for All Occasions 61

2500 Jokes to Start 'Em Laughing 104, 115

10,000 Jokes, Toasts & Stories 36

14,000 Quips and Quotes for Writers and Speakers 45, 103

A

Adams, Joey 13, 109

Allen, Fred 21

Allen, Gracie 114

Allen, Harry 22

Allen, Steve 36, 40, 91

Allen, Woody 116, 118

Alpern, Hyman 22, 24, 34, 82

Apple a Day Perpetual Calendar, An 14, 16

Aronin, Michael 113

Asimov Laughs Again 27

Asimov, Isaac 27

Avalon 46

B

Bacall, Aaron 103

Bankhead, Tallulah 117

Barry, Dave 81, 87, 91

Beamguard, Betty 50

Becquet.com 26, 35, 39, 52, 59, 62, 67, 70

Berle, Milton 21, 23, 63, 114, 116

Bierce, Ambrose 87

Bigger, Margaret G. 55

Biggest Joke Book in the World 37

Bishop, Joey 113

Blank, Eva 30, 93, 101

Bok, Derek 23

Breeden, Vanessa 72

Breeding as a Sport: 101 Student Howlers 33, 38, 59

Bryan, William J. 90

Bumper sticker 44

C

Capper's Weekly 65
Carlin, George 44
Carroll, Lewis 45
Carvey, Dana 47
Cavanaugh, Tim 118
Cerf, Bennett 9, 58
Cho, Margaret 13
Clayton, Joan 59, 65, 72
Complete Speaker's Galaxy of Funny Stories, Jokes and Anecdotes 47, 57, 81, 105
Copeland, Faye 36
Copeland, Louis 36
Cooperberg, Dave 48
Cosby, Bill 37, 39, 42, 47

D

Dangerfield, Rodney 32
DeGeneres, Ellen 113
Del Vecchio, Lisa 60
Denson, Judy Moon 34, 56, 71
Dent, James 96

Dentinger, Ron 77, 90
Detorie, Rick 12, 77, 107
Diller, Phyllis 29, 48
Drucker, Peter 92
Dumas, Alexander 23

E

Enns, Veronica 71
Essmann, Jeffrey 115
Evans, Bergen 90

F

Farmer, Debbie 53
Fechtner, Leopold 47
Floyd, Katherine T. 66
Franzini, Lou 93
Fuller, Edmund 68, 70

G

Goldberg, Arthur 24
Gould, John 92
Graziano, Rocky 116
Green, Roseanne 30, 93, 101

123

H

Hajdusiewicz, Babs Bell 109
Hansen, Melanie 68
Harrington, Patricia 74
Helitzer, Mel 110
Helmer, Marilyn 45
Higgs, Liz Curtis 56, 60, 62, 73
Housholder, Grace Witwer 51, 75
Howe, Edgar Watson 16
Hutcherson, Warren 66
Hutchins, Robert Maynard 93

J

Jokelopedia 30, 93, 101

K

K., Norman 119
Karrer, Paul 78
Kaufman, Bel 33
Kennedy, Gerald 44
Kerr, Clark 98

Kid Stuff 66, 71, 75
KidSpiration 34, 56, 71
Kindergarten student 60
Kinney, David 30
Kissell, Steve 17
Kolberg, Karen 24
Kurisu, Jane 45

L

Lane, Rita 71
Larry Wilde's Library of Laughter 65
Lebowitz, Fran 117
Lederer, Richard 29, 38, 74, 80, 82, 85, 102
Leno, Jay 66, 83
Lewis, Richard 119
Leo Rosten's Giant Book of Laughter 50
Levenson, Sam 17, 100, 104, 112
Levinson, Barry 46
Linkletter, Art 27

124

Loomans, Diane 24
Lundberg, Elaine 15
Lundholm, Mark 114

M

McKenzie, E. C. 45, 103
Mickins, Beverly 47
Miles, Martha 55
Milton Berle's Private Joke File 21, 3, 63, 114, 116
MotherHoot 55
Moulton, Powers 61
Myers, James E. 67

N

Nelson's Big Book of Laughter 61
Newell, Karl 48
Novak, William 100

O

Ohanian, Susan 16
Orben, Robert 16, 89, 104, 105, 115, 117
Otis, Harry B. 73

Page, Lou 18
Pendleton, Winston K. 47, 57, 81, 105
Penguin Dictionary of Jokes, The 115
Perret, Gene 23
Peterson, Art 12, 18, 21
Peterson, Valeka 52
Prochnow, Herbert 117

Quinn, Donald D. 25

R

Random House Book of Jokes and Anecdotes, The 79
Recess Riddles 45
Rich, Roberta 75
Rissinger, Matt 37
Ritchie, Raelyn 109
Rivers, Joan 44
Robertson, Jeanne 97

125

Rosenbloom, Joseph 26, 31, 44, 63, 103
Rosten, Leo 50
Rovin, Jeff 31
Rudin, Helen 31
Rudner, Rita 118

S

Sales, Soupy 76
Scheu, Ted 86, 101
Seeger, Pete 23
Seinfeld, Jerry 114
Shade, Richard A. 108
Singer, Jen 63
Smallwood, Beverly 34, 56, 71
Stark, Judith Frost 72
Steve Allen's Private Joke File 36, 40, 91
Stokes, Grace 54
Streiker, Lowell D. 61

T

Teachers Are Funny 22, 24, 34

Teachernet.com 71
Teachers.Net/chatboard 20, 67, 68
TeachersZine.com 14, 39, 41, 102
Thurston, Cheryl Miller 69
Tooper, Virginia 80
True, Herb 22
Twain, Mark 18, 25

V

Vanaria, Tony 78

W

Wagner, Jane 49, 69
Wake, Lesley 23
Waldoks, Moshe 100
Warning! Cute Kid Stories Ahead! 28, 57, 75
Weitzman, Ilana 30, 93, 101
Wilde, Larry 65
Williams, Robin 119
Wood, David 90

World According to Kids, The
  38, 51

Yates, Philip 37
Yordan, Terry 74
Youngman, Henny 56, 114, 116

127